All Glory and All Praise be to God and God alone

In loving Memory of Henry Jones
One of the most intelligent unlettered men of our
time
"Love you Hen"

There are a number of people who I can thank for helping me in my journey, but I will only name a few. I would like to thank my Mother, the pillar in my life, and the one who's tenderness comforted me in my travels in this world. Next there is my beautiful daughter, who is the joy of my life, and the source of my focus. There is my daughters' older brother, my step son whom I love dearly. I would also like to thank Norfolk State University and its facility for the experience of being a student and a post graduate. Earning my bachelors was one of the greatest moments in my life. To everyone else who has assisted me along the way, Thank You and God Bless You.

Sojourn: The Journey Begins

It does not matter where you are at today, but where you will be tomorrow and the day after and five years from now. So put your plan in place and come journey with me to prosperity. These are the words that I live by daily, that regardless of my situation, I must plan ahead and look ahead to a brighter, richer future Even though there may be stumbling blocks in the way and I may need to tweak my plan, I keep striving towards my goal. I think that if people use this as a daily mantra, it will assist in helping them stay on course to reach their goal, especially when the journey seems like you are at the bottom of Mount Everest, and you have to climb to the peak and you've never been mountain climbing before. Well guess what, you have to get started somewhere. So you plan how you are going to scale this mountain and as you start out you gain ground, and then you slide back, and then you come across obstacles that you can't figure out how to overcome. You've tried and tried again but you can't gain ground. Time to give up; "hey, you gave it all you had and came up with zero", pat yourself on the back and please don't kill what little self-esteem you have left with feeling sorry for yourself, have a beer or glass of wine to chase those blues away. **WRONG ANSWER, YOU HEAR ME, NEVER GIVE UP, NEVER!!** The only time that you stop going after what you want is when you take your last breath, then it will not matter anyway, but I guarantee you will be happy knowing you lived your life the way you wanted versus not going after what you want because it seems impossible, and burying your head in the sand for fear of failure. This is the reason writing this book gives me great joy because I'm just like you or even worse. I've lost my job of eight years that paid me, okay. I've been going through a divorce and custody fight for almost five years, I have no savings. What I got from my job when I left, I had to use to keep a roof over my head, I'm over weight, but you know what, I'm staring this mountain down and I'm saying, I'm going to reach the top and master you buddy. I am going to continue learning about money and finances and create wealth. I have a college degree. I am going to have a regular relationship with my daughter, and I am going to lose weight to be here for her no matter how many times I have a snack that I shouldn't have. I keep moving forward and re-disciplining myself. That's why I say put your plan in place and come journey with me to prosperity, because that's what it is, a road trip through life that leads to the same place sooner or later. So live your life ambitiously and here's a little secret, as with that obstacle on the mountain that you couldn't figure out, if you keep at it, eventually you will solve the problem. It gets even better than that, on this same mountain there are climbers more skilled then you that will see your effort and hard work and will want to help you, assist you, and even offer to team up with you in climbing that mountain. From that point, as long as you stay serious and dedicated, you will successfully reach the top. I can hear your mountain now as you read this book shaking and cracking with fear of your will of determination and steadfastness.

Earlier, I stated some of what my mountain was made of, now I want to share with you what I am climbing towards to reach the peak. I am starting an investment club, I plan to venture into real estate. I have my own investments in the stock market, and I am writing this book and once it is completed and published, I will be an established author. They are all things to be proud of, and these are not all of my goals that I have set for myself. These goals and plans may change, but one plan that I am determined to make happen is that within ten years my investments will be at a point where I don't have to punch anyone's clock, and my business interests will be my full time source of income, and within another 10 years or sooner, I will be able to retire. I think 20 years is enough time for any serious dedicated person to reach their financial goals. Some may say, but I'm forty or fifty, twenty years to become financially free is a long time to wait at my age. Here's my response, "so what are you going to do? accept where your at and say it's to late". I'll tell you what, your riches may come sooner if you are just that smart and or fortune smiles upon you, however, if not, then I say I'd rather be a sixty or seventy year old rich person than a sixty or seventy year old person struggling financially. That's why I say, it's not about right here right now, its about putting your building blocks in place to build your ideal future.

Wealth Consciousness

Becoming rich, being rich, and staying rich is all under the umbrella of being wealthy. You have to 1st have wealth of mind, wealth of spirit, and wealth of emotions in order to gain and secure whatever monetary or financial objective that you believe fits into your puzzle. In other words you have to truly love yourself and be happy with who you are and where you are at right now in life. When your state of mind embraces all these characteristics, you will be in a harmonious state of being and this transient way of life can unlock doors that you desire. Individuals who obtain this level are confident self reliant, patient, determined, positive, and optimistic. To be honest, you probably have some of these traits and know other people who display some of these qualities, but to know or see someone who has all three aspects of wealth conciseness is rare. I once knew a guy like that. I was working at 7-11after I had graduated from college and was looking for another job. This guy was so upbeat and positive nothing could tear him down. I remember telling him that my job hunt was going slow and he would recommend all these jobs unrelated to my Degree. I would say " the jobs you are telling me that are hiring are not related to my field of study. He would respond " you have a degree, you're an educated man there's no such thing as being unqualified because if you can go to college and master a school of discipline then you can go into any career be trained and function. While working at 7-11 we, would spend the entire time conversing about the infinite possibilities that existed and I would challenge him on many topics to see what his response would be, and Mr. positive never missed a beat. I really enjoyed working with him and you would think that everyone else would as well, but to the contrary, everyone that worked with us could not stand him or I would say understand him. A key difference between him and the rest of the crew was that they lived in a world of practicality, wherein his world of being practical was for the above average and the good things of the world were his for the earning. If you want to know what happened to him he had goals of joining the coast guard. Again everyone doubted his ambition and several weeks later he walked in with his coast guard uniform on and that was the last time I saw him.

Wealth of mind, spirit, and emotion, wealth consciousness brings out the noblest and brightest qualities in a person. It gives vision not only to see the world as it is, but also how it can be and will be. There are many people who have the trappings of the "well to do" but are not wealthy or rich in spirit and self-esteem. There are many people who think lots of money can cure ailments of insecurities about ones self, in many cases money perpetuates these issues. Don't believe me look at Wall Street and what extreme greed brings you, over leveraged companies that almost brought this country to its knees, causing some innocent investors and retired people to lose a lot if not all their savings. Think of the many entertainers who had and lost fortunes in the 90's, and anyone will tell you that business will eat you up. I would say that Mike Tyson is the perfect example of what happens to someone who is unbalanced in mind, spirit, and emotions. This man was worth 300 to 400 million dollars about twenty years ago and that amount of money was worth more than it is today because the dollar could purchase more than what it can today. Today, Mike Tyson net value is not even a fraction of what it was. Unfortunately, the balance in life that he needed was not there and his wealth was squandered, mismanaged and stolen. So the next question is how to I obtain wealth consciousness and my answer is one day at a time. No book, no person, can instantaneously make you whole! Although there are tools such as books, tapes, cd's and coaches that can assist and encourage you on your journey to prosperity. For me my 1st step is to ask God to guide, bless and forgive me for mistakes on this road that I'm traveling along. Secondly, its time to look in the mirror and do a serious self analysis. You have to be honest with yourself, not everyone else, yourself. This is about your growth. In this examination, you have to see all your positives and all your opportunities. I prefer opportunities over negatives because seeing things in your character as a challenge to overcome is easier to grasp and take hold of versus looking at oneself negatively which can be emotionally draining and depressing, especially when objectives are not reached in ones development. A person who has wealth consciousness welcomes a challenge and embraces the learning experiences. They also know that perfection is not possible even though they strive to be perfect in all aspects of life gaining mastery over an array of areas. From the arts, to business, finance, science, love making etcetera. Whatever you seek to change or improve on do your homework, put your plan in place and tirelessly work towards your goal and continue to read and learn and evaluate and reevaluate your strengths and opportunities.

There is a very interesting interview I found on the internet at spirituality.com that deals with controlling the mind and why we have impulses and compulsions. These impules can cause us to do things that are not always in our best interest. For instance, why do I continue to max out my credit cards or why can't I stick to my budget, I always feel guilty about the amount of money I pay for an item. Dr. Pandit states that "the mind is driven by the senses and that the senses crave the pleasures of the external world and the focus on these objects good or bad give momentary euphoria". Dr. Pandit explains that once the mind realizes the emptiness of the experience, the senses drive the mind to look to the external world for pleasure and what you constantly have is a revolving door between unhappiness and sensory pleasure. The mind therefore becomes frustrated and is in a constant state of turmoil for lack of satisfaction and peace. This rings true in how we view ourselves in relation to our world. For instance, I feel down, let me binge on junk food, after thought, I feel worse now; or I'll go shopping with the same results, Buying to much house or car to feel important or good, then the reality kicks in when the mortgage and car payments have to be met, and the mind becomes stressed at the monthly financial burden. To further understand this Dr. Pandit states that "the mind creates value in the external world" and I will take it one step further to say that those who control entertainment, and culture dictate to the masses what is valuable in this world and in turn you have people reaching to obtain the material possessions of those at the top versus taking the necessary steps to become part of the top.

While controlling the mind is important and once on this track or even mastering it, realizing the possibilities of creativity is next. Another article I found on the internet called The power of the mind is very inspirational and hones in on many points of this chapter. That is why I include part of it in this book. Notice I have underlined several phrases in the article. <u>The article starts with your thoughts create your reality. That which you focus on creates your reality. That which you focus on is what you attract to yourself. If you are unhappy with your life, find one thing you like and concentrate on it. You get what you concentrate on. If someone is making you happy your focusing on it if someone is making you mad your focusing on it. No one makes you feel anything, your feelings are as much a choice as anything else. This is why forgiveness is important it frees you from focusing on something negative and does nothing for the other person your angry at. If you can accept that your life is your own creation, that everything is created by your thoughts, then your ready for conscious abundance creation. If you want a life of wealth, health and prosperity choose that life, claim it. Through his thoughts, man holds the key to every situation and contains within himself that transforming and regenerative agency by which he may make himself what he wills. As a man thinketh James Allen</u>

Wealth

Now that the psychological and spiritual are in place or being put in place, what's next? You are ready to be wealthy, meaning you want to have more than enough money to do pretty much whatever it is you want when you want among other things. I think the best approach to this is to understand what the word wealth means. Wealth is the abundance of resources and materials. This means that you have a massive amount of ownership of something, or in something, that can be utilized to put money in your pocket For instance you could own 50,000 acres of land. You are land wealthy. The next question is " how do I put the land to work to generate income for me?" The above example should give you a better understanding of what wealth is, but since you might not have 50,000 acres of land now what? I know you most likely have read a number of books that were informative and inspiring (which I pray that this book provides those same feelings) but left you wondering what is my next step. I have written this book with the intention of answering that question. I am not going to instruct you as to what to do or how to do it, that is for you to decide, but what I will do is give you two undeniable paths to being wealthy that should be life changing. We are also going to challenge your perception of money and how it works and what its worth.

Remember how wealth was defined. (Wealth is the abundance of resources and materials). Within the term wealth exists two roads that lead to becoming wealthy. Knowing which road to take will be crucial to your success. The paths are Wealth Creation and Creation of Wealth. I'm sure you are thinking that I took these two words and just switched them around. I assure you that it is deeper than that. For one, when you change words around, you can change the meaning of that word or phrase. Second, there is power in words so always choose your words wisely. Wealth creation is the utilization of wealth (abundance of resources and materials) already in place and structured to generate revenue and income. Anyone can apply this strategy but it is commonly used by people we call investors. They look for great businesses or start-ups and infuse them with cash (capitol) for ROI (Return on Investment). In essence, they give companies money to run their business and in return the company shares a percentage of their profits with them. The alternative path is called creation of wealth. This road starts with an idea or concept to make money and the individuals have to assemble the materials and resources needed to start their business. The idea or concept can be original or it can be an improvement or enhancement to an existing business model. Wealth creation and creation of wealth are two distinct concepts, however, you will notice that many business men are investors and many investors are business owners.

The perfect examples of wealth creation and creation of wealth is Warren Buffet and Bill Gates. These two men are the richest men in the world. Bill Gates is the owner of Microsoft and accumulated his wealth based on his software development. We can agree that he created his wealth from being a co-inventor of Microsoft. Warren Buffet is the second richest man in the world. He made his billions investing in other companies and in businesses where he saw value that others did not. Both of these men took different but similar routes to achieve massive amounts of wealth. The reason why they are different is because Bill Gates created Microsoft, Warren Buffet invested in and brought great companies, which in turn makes them similar even though Mr. Buffet did not start a service business, he still has controlling interest in other companies, which make him a business owner. Bill Gates the owner of Microsoft invest in other companies and new technologies which makes him an investor. Therefore, in both cases the lines have crossed.

Starting Point/The Path

In Robert Kiyosaki book "Rich Dad Poor Dad" (a great read) he places people into four groups.. There are the E's for employees, the S's for self-employed, the I's for investor and the B's for business owners. Robert Kiyosaki gives a fantastic break down for each group but emphasizes that if you want to be rich, you need to be in the B (business owner) or I (investor) categories to be rich or as I would say wealthy. When I read this my next question was okay now how do I do this in the category for employee. Immediately my mind went to everything that prevented me from moving to the next category. I was an employee, I did not have any connections or relationships that could assist me, and I did not have any capital to launch anything of significance. So what do I do now? I contemplated this for many months and a couple of years. The answer finally came to me simple and as plain as day, You have to start from somewhere. So reflecting back on Robert Kiyosaki's four groups , I envisioned my path and how it should look or my road to wealth through wealth creation and creation of wealth. As an employee, I have to start from E and as I go down that road it comes to a fork or divide and their two paths that I can take and one path is as an investor , the other path is as a self-employed individual or a business owner, and that regardless of what path I took these two roads would soon intertwine.

As you can see, being an employee sooner or later if I want wealth, I have to make a decision on how I plan to obtain it. I am going to take the investor path. I am going the investor road and the self-employed road and if I travel far enough all these paths will intertwine and become one. With this in mind, you have to start from wherever you are at, how you start is up to you.
An example of what you can do is obtain an online account. Sharebuilder is an online site where you can buy stocks and does not require a lot of money to get started, then as you progress and learn more you can become more aggressive and invest or day trade with other sites that have more freedom to trade and invest without limits.

Once you purchase a share of stock outside of your 401k, you have taken your monumental step in becoming an investor. If you want to become a business owner or self-employed then do it. There are a number of things you can do or sell. There are oils, candles, incense, fragrance and so on and so forth that you can market to the public. You can start a landscaping business or garbage removal business, you may say this has already been done. You don't have to try these businesses, and secondly just because its being done, the question is can you do it and market it better than the others in this field. To gain customers and market share you have to work on improving the quality of the service or product that you are providing to the consumer beyond their present expectations. If you have an original idea have you put it on paper? have you worked on making it better? have you tried to position yourself around people who can assist you in bringing your idea to life? One of the most important resources in acquiring wealth is building relationships and friendships with those who are actually doing the same thing you are. You can join your local small business administration and chamber of commerce among other institutions. These organizations offer seminars and mentorship's that will be helpful. Wealth can come quickly and wealth may have to be amassed over a period of time. This depends on you, either way continue up the road of wealth creation and creation of wealth until you make it to your destination. You paint the picture for your destiny.

PlayPlay Money/ Playing The Money Game

Money is a game in the business arena but it is a serious game and a game for keeps. There are winners and losers in the money game, however, the people who understand the rules of the game win more then they lose. The first thing I want to address about money is that it has no value. You will hear people say the value of paper money is going down because the Federal Reserve is printing to much and flooding the market. You will also here about putting money back on the gold standard, which is supposed to increase its value. I am going to restate what I said earlier money has no value in and of itself. If you provide a service that has value because you are doing something that creates a convenience for someone else. A product also has value for example a microwave, laptop, car, cell phone and so on. Gold and silver have value they are used in many of the devices we use today. Gold and silver were also the 1st form of currency and the merchant had to weigh the silver and gold for payment. With paper money you do none of these things. The government prints 1,5,10.20,50, and 100 on paper money and says this is what it is worth. Our system uses this monetary matrix to assess price point to services, products and labor technological skills. Money is only a means to measure the worth of a product and service. It is also a medium between businesses and between consumers and businesses for products and services. Thus, paper money has no value and is a medium for trade. A dollar today is a dollar tomorrow. One important aspect of the dollar is its purchasing power. The purchasing power of the dollar has been falling for years as the price for goods and services rise. Therefore, you need more dollars to trade for things of value. The strength of the dollar is backed by its government, if the government is strong the dollar is strong, if the government is weak the dollar is weak. This analysis also applies to the measuring of purchasing power of other foreign currencies against our own (Watch China). My main reason for focusing on the value of money versus its purchasing power is to have you understand not to get entangled with how many dollars you have, but how many assets, products, and services that you own or are looking to own that will pay you dollars every week, month, and quarter, or year. This is what will make you wealthy and keep you wealthy. Remember the rich receive large checks the wealthy write large checks.

People who are wealthy are wealthy for a reason, be it inventor or investor. The wealthy and the rich speak the language of money, they go to the same social spots, and they belong to many of the same for profit and charitable organizations.

The wealthy never go at it alone or do anything by themselves. They have a host of professionals working along side them. They have attorneys on retainer, stock brokers, personal assistants and many other representatives who assist them in maintaining and growing their assets. These group of advisors report to the wealthy and respond and take action for the wealthy when needed or requested. Even though you may not have the money to acquire this kind of support, you can put alerts on your different accounts be it checking or credit report among other things. It is also free to go in and develop a relationship with your banks representatives. You can set up appointments to see an account manager or the branch manager. Banks have specialty departments that deals with loans, debt management and other financials. You can go in and talk with them and get information regarding financing, budgeting, and investing. There are attorneys who will let you pay them a monthly fee to retain them. You can work out the details when you meet with them, obtain an agreement on a list of services they will provide. Wealth is the abundance of resources and relationships are definitely an important resource.

The saying goes that knowledge is power, I say that knowledge is strength because it is the ability to do. Wisdom is power because it is the application of knowledge. Knowledge means nothing if you don't or can't use it to your advantage. Once you apply what you know you gain a better understanding of what you already have knowledge of, which in turn causes you to become wiser and more efficient. You can have knowledge of how to start a business, invest in the stock market or even ride a bicycle, however, if you have never done it before that knowledge is fruitless. You may need to get across town quickly and all you have is a bicycle. You know it has handle bars, peddles and a seat and it is a quicker form of transportation than walking, but if you have never rode a bike you won't get across town. It would be better to walk or find a ride. In other words, you have to work at perfecting your craft, art and or business skills. There are some distinct characters that I would like to touch on regarding being successful in business or any project. You don't have to be a prodigy or even exceptionally gifted to do great and wonderful things. What you do have to have is a desire to learn and vision. Vision not only to see the present but the future of what can be. Everyone has a brain but a mind is something that needs to be developed. A human brain functions on basic needs such as hunger, fear, happiness an other carnal wants, however, when it comes to dealing with opportunities` on crisis situations the brain will shut down or revert to an animal way of responding. A mind is the brain being trained and able to function on a higher level of perception. By being educated or educating yourself, you can soar to a level were you access the higher faculties of the mind. In this state the mind has a heightened awareness and can understand, solve and give probable outcomes to situations. This is called intelligence. There is a difference between being intelligent and being smart. You can be smart but not intelligent. I define smart as being able to process, retain and regurgitate information. Some people are smarter then others and I know some people who are very smart but who don't have a lick of common sense, meaning they don't handle decision making processes well. There are some people who are smart and intelligent and when you are around them you know it and you can sense it in there aura. These individuals have it together all the way around and are a major assets to there community. Warren Buffet would be a prime example, he is a tough business man and good natured Samaritan. He does not represent one extreme or another, he is very centered and balanced.

Be The King Of Yourself, Be The king Of Your Destiny.

There are 3 instruments that you will need to get you to your goal. They are commitment, drive, the way. Once all three of these character traits are combined and implemented, success whether instantaneous or distant is assuredly guaranteed. You must have a solid foundation. You must be undeterred and committed to your unwavering goal. Commitment will push through any rejections, obstacles and dilemmas that might slow you or temporarily derail your plans. Drive will speed you up the road of success to your objective. Drive is the fuel that causes you to accomplish priorities on the road to prosperity. As you move forward, your mind is always processing what moves you have made and which moves need to be executed next. Having the drive to keep pushing will force you to keep coming up with ideas and trying them. Your drive has to be an unstoppable force of nature. The way is the direction you decide to follow that will bring you the outcome you are expecting. Some will know specifically what the way is for them others will have to find their mojo. Starting out you may try several different ventures until your find you niche. Then your way, your path to wealth is set. Remember wealth is not only about an abundance of resources and materials, it is about an assurance of self worth and self value mentally, spiritually, and physically. To love yourself and to love others in the process and to understand those who do not understand you or themselves.

Keep yourself motivated and stay around people who are motivated. Positive people give you positive charge. Negative people give a negative charge and can drain your battery, affecting your commitment and drive to your goal, at the same time you need to understand the difference between constructive criticism and deconstructive criticism. Deconstructive criticism tries to kill your dream by offering every reason why you can't accomplish your goals. Constructive criticism will point out weak spots in your plan and suggest ways to fix it and make it better. Never be around or take advice from someone who always focuses on the negative. Another way to stay positively charged is to read books about what you want to do, watch television programs, and listen to tapes centered on your passion. You will then begin to develop a list of authors and subject matters that impact you the most. You will identify with different authors for different reasons. Many people have been where you are at and have communicated their stories of overcoming the odds through different forms of communication. Surround yourself with what you want to become and you will become just that.

Here is a list of authors and books that have inspired me and continue to inspire me. The more I read and read these books the more I get from them every time.

Robert Kiyosaki "Rich Dad, Poor Dad: A guide to investing"

Michael Masterson "Automatic Wealth for Grads… and Anyone Else Just Starting Out"

Robert G. Hagstrom, Kenneth L. Fisher and Bill Mille "The Buffet Way"

Wealth Of Knowledge

I believe one great aspect in me writing this book is that I am writing it from the perspective of someone who is not rich. Most books are from authors who have already amassed a certain amount of wealth, while my book is written during my journey to success and it is a fresh look at what it takes to make it. I have made progress from the beginning of the book until now. I am currently seeking my masters in Business Administration with a concentration in Entrepreneurship. I was a manager for the world's largest retailer and was part of a team operating a one hundred million store. I currently work for a credit card company as an account manager. I assist account holders with their lines of credit. I help them understand their different annual APR'S on their line of credit, wherein there are four of them. I transfer money from their lines of credit to pay off other credit cards and loans. Credit card holders can also draft money directly into their checking account from their card and sometimes at a zero percent interest rate for a year with a promotional offer. Credit cards can be used to pay for vacations, buy cars, expand or start a business and even purchase a home.

Having or rebuilding a good credit score is very important. Here are some tricks you can use to increase your credit score. Build a relationship with your bank, ask for a small loan, the bank may want collateral to secure your loan. You will need something of value as the guarantor of the loan, for example a vehicle that you own the title to. If and when the bank gives you the loan, you will have to be disciplined enough not to spend it. Use that same money to repay the bank loan. You will most likely pay the last installment loan out of pocket. The bank will report to the credit bureau that you have paid your loan in a timely manner and have paid off the account in good standing. This will raise your credit score and will open the door for you to go back to the bank and ask for an unsecured loan for real purchases. The better your payment history the more available credit they will extend you. Another way to build your credit score is to leave a positive or over payment on loans and lines of credit that report to the credit bureaus. When they report to the credit bureau on your account they will report that they owe you money. Limit and monitor companies whom you do business with because every time they pull your report it brings down your score. Even if you have good or great credit, watch your income to debt ratio, consumers with high revolving debt can be considered risky debtors.

My personal experience with being a business owner on the road to wealth encompasses a few ventures. I have run an eatery out of two night clubs with a partner. We took turns operating the eatery on opposite weekends and I will tell you it feels great to receive income while not having to do anything physically to earn it. I am starting an assembly business and I also invest in the stock market. I still plan to start my investment group and invest in real estate. There are also some other ventures I am thinking about trying but I am not taking it to seriously and you shouldn't either. Life is short and the journey is long and in this life our destination is the same whether rich or poor, so enjoy the journey. Take time out for yourself and your loved ones, laugh as much as you can, find humor in things that trouble you, and free your mind. Trust me, in the true reality, money has no more value than a piece of notebook paper, the tree that it was produced from has more value and worth, so take the time out to appreciate and thank God, for life truly is a gift.

I would like to thank you for purchasing this book and I pray that it is a source of enlightenment and motivation for you. If you would like to continue on this journey with me and assist others on this sojourn you can join us @OpulentV on twitter & SageSojourner on Youtube.